Welcome to your we~~~, ~ Intention...

Hi, my name is Janetta Olaseni and I am revealing to you in this journal some of my P.O.P. strategies. To P.O.P. means to Prosper On Purpose.
To live from the inside out intentionally. Intentions are powerful because they come from within. By setting a daily intention we are walking in our purpose, not by surprise but by FAITH! Living with intention allows us to respond to situations as they arrive instead of reacting (preparation is never lost time).
I have not always lived intentionally...
I've been caught off guard by ups and downs, disappointments, sickness, and valleys.
But there is one thing that has remained a constant force in my life "The Lord." My prayer is that this journal will help you to P.O.P. In your spirit, mind, health, relationships and your finances.

J. Olaseni

RN/BC-HN/CHC
www.JanettaHolisticRN.com

How to use:

For each week there is an area of focus (spirit, mind, health, relationships, and finances) and a scripture that you may read and meditate on.
Underneath the scripture to the left there is a place for you to free text any goals for the week.
To the right there is a free text space for Wins (what you have accomplished.)
There is also a space for personal application.
This is where you may want to see yourself in the scriptures.
Ex: Death and Life are in the power of the tongue. Prov 18:21a
Personal Application: Lord I thank you that I choose life and today I'm walking in love and power!
Mon-Sun days with lines for your intentional notes.
What are your to do's?
What do you need to remember?
At the end of the week there is an extra space for note taking (favorite book quotes, studies, church, etc...) Coloring is said to unlock creativity and increase focus.
These coloring pages represent different careers and goals (color the vision.)
Remember it's about making small shifts day after day that create massive shifts in our lives.

*** Meditation in the Bible means reflective thinking on biblical truth so that God is able to speak to us through Scripture and through the thoughts that come to mind as we are reflecting on the Word, but that must also be filtered by the Word.

*Scriptures used in this journal are coming from the King James Version of the Bible unless otherwise noted.

P.O.P. ™

Prosper On Purpose

Tips to Self-Discovery

How well do you really know yourself? Have you ever taken the time to listen to what your life is telling you about your true nature?

It's okay if you haven't. Few of us ever make time for intentional self-discovery. We're bombarded with messages from other people—what they think of us, how they perceive us, what they want for us—that we forget to include the one voice that matters. Our own!

The easiest way to get to know yourself is the same way you would get to know anyone else. **Ask meaningful, personal questions. Interview yourself.**

Record your answers daily or just meditate and follow some deep breathing techniques in my blog post here: **Http://bit.ly/POPBreathe.**

1. What is your favorite physical characteristic (face or body)? Describe a time you felt proud of that feature.
2. What physical characteristics are you most self-conscious about? How could you make peace with those?
3. What is your greatest strength? Describe a time this strength served you well.
4. What is your greatest weakness? Describe a time this weakness held you back.
5. Describe a time you felt especially valued and loved.
6. Finish this sentence: "I can't stand it when other people..." Examine those character flaws. Do you also possess them? Be honest.
7. Today is your first day at your dream job. You're so excited you can barely contain yourself. When you arrive at work, you take a minute to look around and appreciate the moment. You can't believe you actually got this job. Where are you? Why do you value this job so much?
8. Name a book that spoke to you on a personal level. Why?
9. If you had a theme song, what would it be?
10. Name an animal whose characteristics you admire. Are you in any way like that animal?
11. What do you enjoy most about your favorite hobby? How can incorporate that into other parts of your life?

12. Describe a day in your life that was especially enjoyable. What made the day so good?
13. When you think about your future, what do you fear the most?
14. When you think about your future, what do you hope for the most?
15. Describe a time you mistreated someone. How do you feel about your behavior, and what would you say to the person now?
16. Write about a missed opportunity you had taken. What could you do differently next time?
17. What do you look for in a close friend? Do you have those characteristics?
18. Describe a time a friend went out of their way to help you. How do you serve the people in your life?
19. Are you a spiritual person? Describe your beliefs and/or doubts. How do those beliefs affect how you live your life?
20. Discuss how the people in your life make you feel. How do you perceive yourself after spending time with them? How will that affect how you spend time with them in the future?
21. True or False: "I know how to stick up for myself." Explain your answer.
22. You just moved in to your dream home. Look out the kitchen window. What do you see?
23. Your neighbors are having a party. You only know 1 person who is attending. Will you go to the party?
24. You just spent all day by yourself. Are you bored?
25. You've just met a stranger at a place you frequent. He/she tells you a bit about his/her life. Are you listening intently? Or are you waiting for an opening to talk about yourself? Neither answer is incorrect. Describe how this meeting made you feel.
26. You just spent a day at the beach. How do you feel? Energized? Tired? Alternatively, you spent a day in the mountains. How do you feel?
27. You're in an elevator and someone you admire walks in. Do you give the person your business card? Why or why not?
28. To show someone you love them, are you likely to use words, actions, or another method?
29. You've just started working at a new job. One of your colleagues is mean/unkind to you. How do you handle the situation?

30. You walk into a white room filled with white furniture. Does it feel clean or sterile? What does this tell you about the rest of your home. Imagine the room with colorful walls and colorful furniture. How does this change your feelings?
31. Someone gives you a complex task you're not sure how to accomplish. Do you make a plan? Ask someone for help? Research how others have done similar projects in the past? Read a book on the topic. What does this tell you about your learning style?
32. Do you lean into challenge or away from it? Describe a time you were given a challenge you weren't sure you could complete. How did the situation make you feel?
33. Someone trusts you with a secret and asks you not to reveal it. It's really juicy! Do you tell anyone?
34. A colleague takes credit for your work and is rewarded. How does that affect your perception of your own value? How do you react?
35. You are walking on a road, and you encounter three forks. One path leads up a mountain. The other leads into a forest. The third path leads to the ocean. Which path do you take? What do you think this means about you?
36. True or False: "I am more likely to try something if others would be impressed."
37. If you have a problem, would you go to a family member, best friend, or a stranger?
38. You're in a room with a group of people who all share the same opinion on a certain topic. Do you go with the flow or argue the counterpoint?
39. Two teams are playing in a big game. One of them is heavily favored to win. Which team do you support?
40. Your to-do list this week is overwhelming. Do you ask for help or give up sleep?
41. A group of people is having a conversation on a topic you know nothing about. One of them turns to you and asks your opinion. Do admit ignorance or bluff your way out?
42. You are on a team of people creating an iconic building. Which job do you want to help with: managing the project, designing the building, ensuring its safety, or final decorations? Why did you pick that job?
43. You can work at a job you love for very little pay, or work at job you hate for a luxurious salary. Which do you take?

44. You partner is not giving you something you need. Do you tell them or suffer in silence?
45. True or False: "All is fair in love and war." Explain your answer in the context of your life.
46. You have an important task to do. Do you do it now or procrastinate?
47. You overhear a stranger giving information/advice you believe is incorrect. Do you correct the person or stay out of it?
48. You are feeling down. What do you do to cheer yourself up?
49. Describe a time you were radiantly happy. What do you value most in that memory?
50. City mouse or country mouse. Which are you?
51. You're on a gameshow that benefits the charity/cause of your choosing. What do you support? Why?
52. You got great news today. Who do you tell first: Your best friend, the first person you see, or social media?

These questions and tips can help you open up to self-analysis and self-reflection, in a kind and self-compassionate way.

So, step onto your new path to prospering on purpose. **YOU certainly are worth it.**

INSTRUCT

ENCOURAGE

PRAISE

INFLUENCE

SHARE

GUIDE

INSPIRE

 **IN** Spirit

JOHN 3:6

That which is born of the flesh is flesh; and that which is born of the Spirit is spirit.

GOALS   WINS

-
-
-
-
-
-
-
-
-
-
-

(personal application)

MONDAY

TUESDAY

WEDNESDAY

THURSDAY

FRIDAY

SATURDAY

SUNDAY

NOTES

 IN Soul

1 Corinthians 10:13

The temptations in your life are no different from what others experience. And God is faithful. He will not allow the temptation to be more than you can stand. When you are tempted, he will show you a way out so that you can endure.

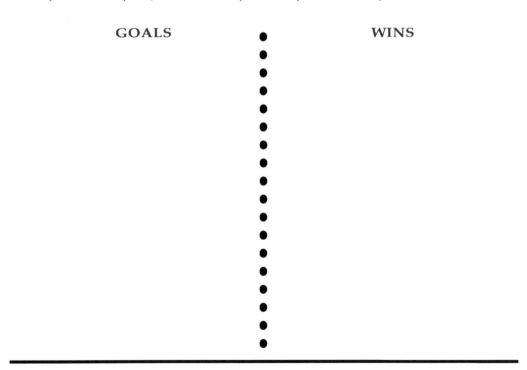

GOALS   WINS

(personal application)

MONDAY

TUESDAY

WEDNESDAY

THURSDAY

FRIDAY

SATURDAY

SUNDAY

NOTES

 **IN** # Health

3 John (AMP) # 1:2

Beloved, I pray that in every way you may succeed and prosper and be in good health [physically], just as [I know] your soul prospers [spiritually].

GOALS   WINS

-
-
-
-
-
-
-
-
-
-
-
-
-
-
-
-
-
-

(personal application)

MONDAY

TUESDAY

WEDNESDAY

THURSDAY

FRIDAY

SATURDAY

SUNDAY

NOTES

 **IN** # Finances

29:11 Jeremiah (NIV)

For I know the plans I have for you, plans to prosper you and not to harm you, plans to give you hope and a future.

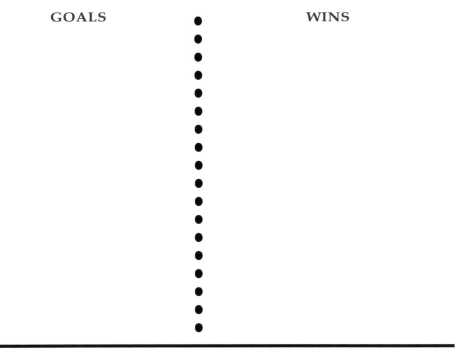

GOALS   WINS

(personal application)

MONDAY

TUESDAY

WEDNESDAY

THURSDAY

FRIDAY

SATURDAY

SUNDAY

NOTES

5:22 Ephesians

Wives, submit yourselves unto your own husbands, as unto the Lord.

GOALS 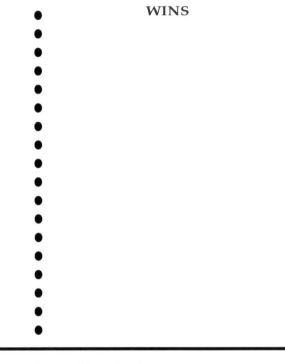 WINS

(personal application)

MONDAY

TUESDAY

WEDNESDAY

THURSDAY

FRIDAY

SATURDAY

SUNDAY

NOTES

"Nurses dispense comfort, compassion, and caring without even a prescription."

P.O.P.
Prosper On Purpose

 **IN Spirit**

8:1 Romans

There is therefore now no condemnation to them which are in Christ Jesus, who walk not after the flesh, but after the Spirit.

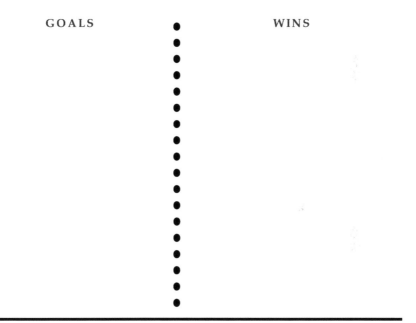

GOALS   WINS

(personal application)

MONDAY

TUESDAY

WEDNESDAY

THURSDAY

FRIDAY

SATURDAY

SUNDAY

NOTES

 IN Soul

1 Corinthians 10:4-5

The weapons of our warfare are not physical [weapons of flesh and blood]. Our weapons are divinely powerful for the destruction of fortresses. We are destroying sophisticated arguments and every exalted and proud thing that sets itself up against the [true] knowledge of God, and we are taking every thought and purpose captive to the obedience of Christ.

GOALS   WINS

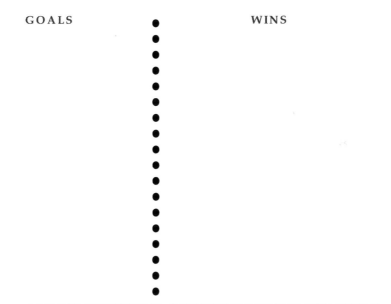

(personal application)

MONDAY

TUESDAY

WEDNESDAY

THURSDAY

FRIDAY

SATURDAY

SUNDAY

NOTES

Prosper On Purpose

IN Health

12:1 Romans

*I beseech you therefore, brethren, by the mercies of God, that ye present
your bodies a living sacrifice, holy, acceptable unto God, which is
your reasonable service.*

GOALS   WINS

(personal application)

MONDAY

TUESDAY

WEDNESDAY

THURSDAY

FRIDAY

SATURDAY

SUNDAY

NOTES

6:38 Luke NLT

Give, and you will receive. Your gift will return to you in full—pressed down, shaken together to make room for more, running over, and poured into your lap. The amount you give will determine the amount you get back.

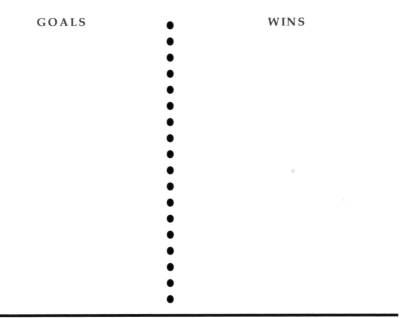

GOALS   WINS

(personal application)

MONDAY

TUESDAY

WEDNESDAY

THURSDAY

FRIDAY

SATURDAY

SUNDAY

NOTES

If you think the pursuit of good health is expensive and time consuming, try illness.

-Lee Swanson

IN **Spirit**

JOHN (NLT) 6:63

The Spirit alone gives eternal life. Human effort accomplishes nothing. And the very words I have spoken to you are spirit and life.

GOALS   WINS

(personal application)

MONDAY

TUESDAY

WEDNESDAY

THURSDAY

FRIDAY

SATURDAY

SUNDAY

NOTES

P.O.P. ™
Prosper On Purpose

IN **Soul**

Romans (NLT)   **12:2**

Don't copy the behavior and customs of this world, but let God transform you into a new person by changing the way you think. Then you will learn to know God's will for you, which is good and pleasing and perfect.

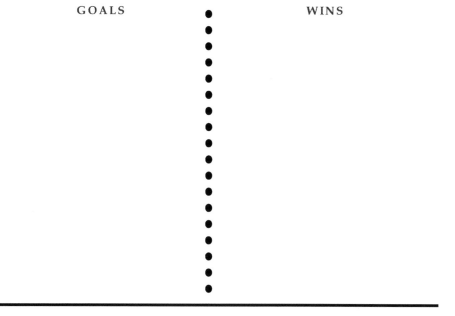

GOALS   WINS

(personal application)

MONDAY

TUESDAY

WEDNESDAY

THURSDAY

FRIDAY

SATURDAY

SUNDAY

NOTES

 IN Health

103:3 Psalms

Who forgiveth all thine iniquities; who healeth all thy diseases;

GOALS 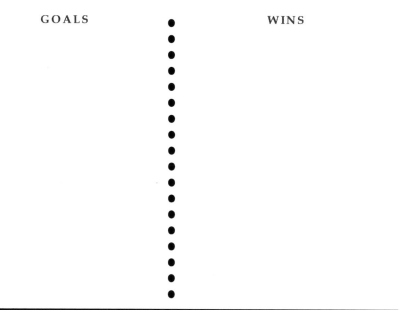 WINS

(personal application)

MONDAY

TUESDAY

WEDNESDAY

THURSDAY

FRIDAY

SATURDAY

SUNDAY

NOTES

IN Finances

11:24 Mark

Therefore, I say unto you, what things so ever ye desire, when ye pray, believe that ye receive them, and ye shall have them.

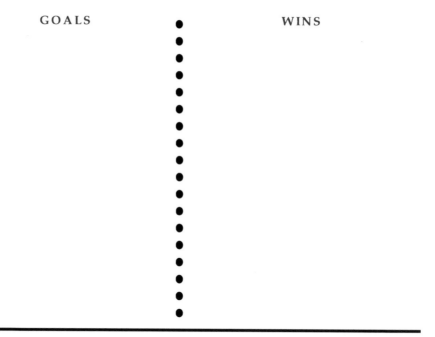

GOALS   WINS

(personal application)

MONDAY

TUESDAY

WEDNESDAY

THURSDAY

FRIDAY

SATURDAY

SUNDAY

NOTES

2 Corinthians 12:9a

And He said unto me, "My grace is sufficient for thee: for my strength is made perfect in weakness".

GOALS · WINS

-
-
-
-
-
-
-
-
-
-
-
-
-
-
-
-
-

(personal application)

MONDAY

TUESDAY

WEDNESDAY

THURSDAY

FRIDAY

SATURDAY

SUNDAY

NOTES

 IN Soul

Proverbs (AMP) 16:3

Commit your works to the Lord [submit and trust them to Him], And your plans will succeed [if you respond to His will and guidance].

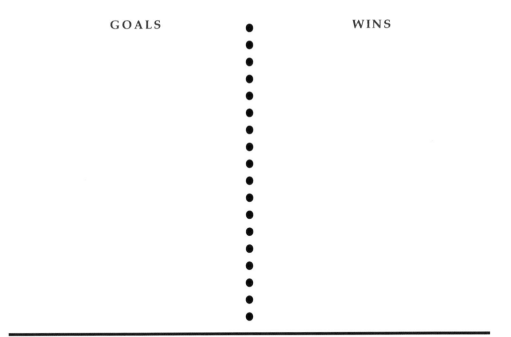

GOALS   WINS

(personal application)

MONDAY

TUESDAY

WEDNESDAY

THURSDAY

FRIDAY

SATURDAY

SUNDAY

NOTES

IN Health

53:5 Isaiah (NLT)

But He was pierced for our rebellion, crushed for our sins. He was beaten so we could be whole. He was whipped so we could be healed.

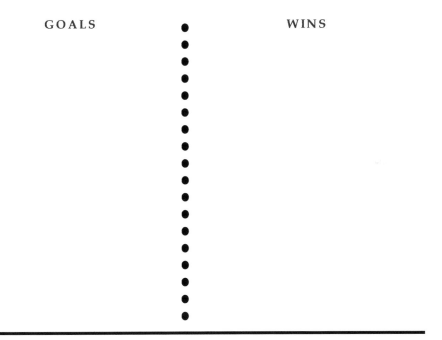

GOALS   WINS

(personal application)

MONDAY

TUESDAY

WEDNESDAY

THURSDAY

FRIDAY

SATURDAY

SUNDAY

NOTES

 IN Finances

28:25 Proverbs (AMP)

An arrogant and greedy man stirs up strife; But he who trusts in the Lord will be blessed and prosper.

GOALS   WINS

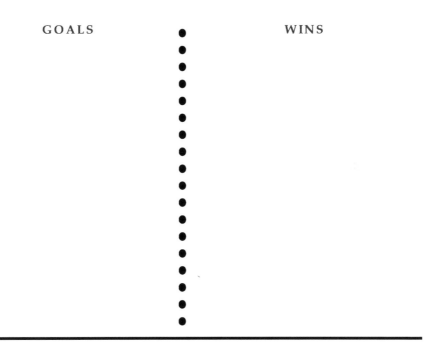

(personal application)

MONDAY

TUESDAY

WEDNESDAY

THURSDAY

FRIDAY

SATURDAY

SUNDAY

NOTES

Single Mom
Point your kids in the right direction—
when they're old they won't be lost. Prov 22:6 MSG

Ephesians 6:2

Honour thy father and mother; (which is the first commandment with a promise;)

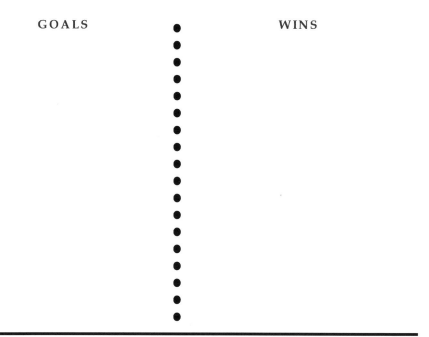

GOALS   WINS

(personal application)

MONDAY

TUESDAY

WEDNESDAY

THURSDAY

FRIDAY

SATURDAY

SUNDAY

NOTES

IN Spirit

Proverbs 18:21a

Death and life are in the power of the tongue: and they that love it shall eat the fruit thereof.

GOALS

WINS

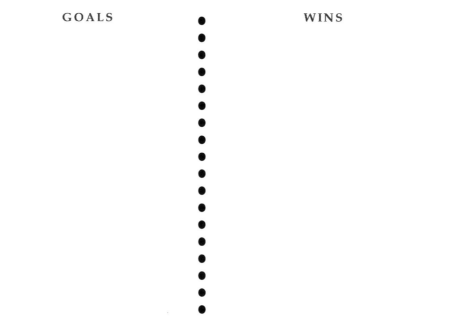

(personal application)

MONDAY

TUESDAY

WEDNESDAY

THURSDAY

FRIDAY

SATURDAY

SUNDAY

NOTES

 IN Soul

53:5 Joshua

This book of the law shall not depart out of thy mouth; but thou shalt meditate therein day and night, that thou mayest observe to do according to all that is written therein: for then thou shalt make thy way prosperous, and then thou shalt have good success.

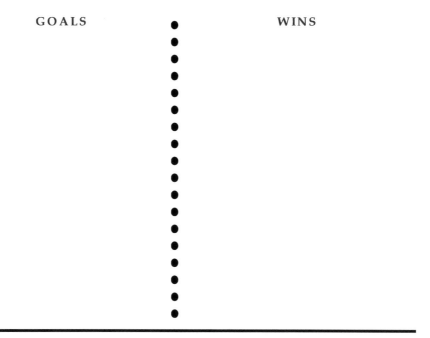

GOALS WINS

(personal application)

MONDAY

TUESDAY

WEDNESDAY

THURSDAY

FRIDAY

SATURDAY

SUNDAY

NOTES

2:24 1 Peter

Who his own self bore our sins in his own body on the tree, that we, being dead to sins, should live to righteousness: by whose stripes you were healed.

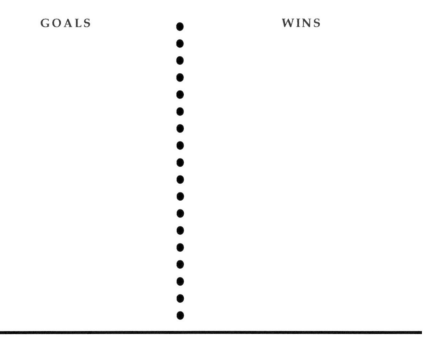

GOALS

WINS

(personal application)

MONDAY

TUESDAY

WEDNESDAY

THURSDAY

FRIDAY

SATURDAY

SUNDAY

NOTES

 IN Finances

6:9 Galatians (GNT)

So let us not become tired of doing good; for if we do not give up, the time will come when we will reap the harvest.

GOALS   WINS

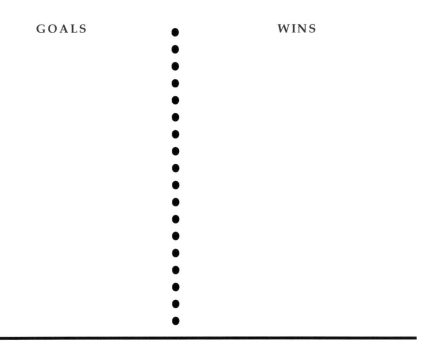

(personal application)

MONDAY

TUESDAY

WEDNESDAY

THURSDAY

FRIDAY

SATURDAY

SUNDAY

NOTES

IN **Spirit**

6:9 2 Corinthians

For we walk by faith, not by sight.

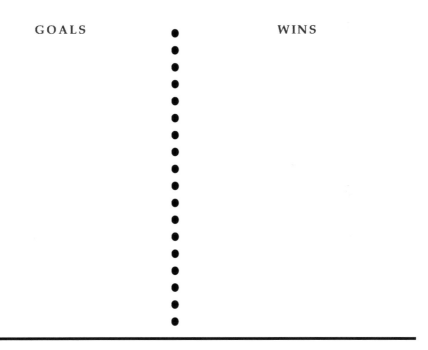

GOALS

WINS

(personal application)

MONDAY

TUESDAY

WEDNESDAY

THURSDAY

FRIDAY

SATURDAY

SUNDAY

NOTES

 **IN** Soul

34:19 Psalms

Many are the afflictions of the righteous: but the LORD delivereth him out of them all.

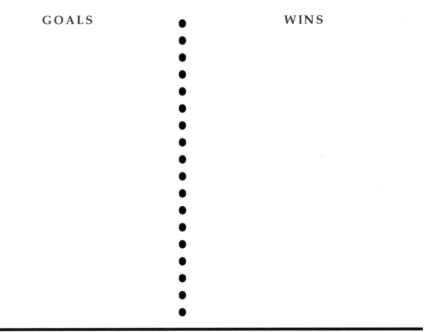

GOALS   WINS

(personal application)

MONDAY

TUESDAY

WEDNESDAY

THURSDAY

FRIDAY

SATURDAY

SUNDAY

NOTES

8:11 Romans

But if the Spirit of him that raised up Jesus from the dead dwell in you, he that raised up Christ from the dead shall also quicken your mortal bodies by his Spirit that dwelleth in you.

GOALS   WINS

(personal application)

MONDAY

TUESDAY

WEDNESDAY

THURSDAY

FRIDAY

SATURDAY

SUNDAY

NOTES

4:19 Philippians

But my God shall supply all your need according to his riches in glory by Christ Jesus.

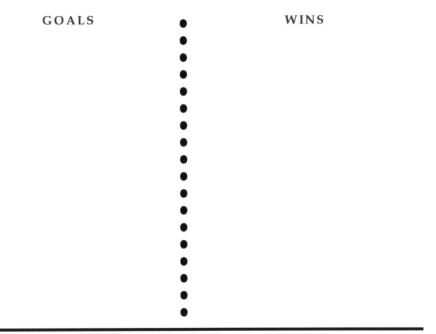

GOALS   WINS

(personal application)

MONDAY

TUESDAY

WEDNESDAY

THURSDAY

FRIDAY

SATURDAY

SUNDAY

NOTES

"The most important thing a father can do for his children is to love their mother."

- Theodore Hesburg

1:3 James (NLT)

*For you know that when your faith is tested,
your endurance has a chance to grow.*

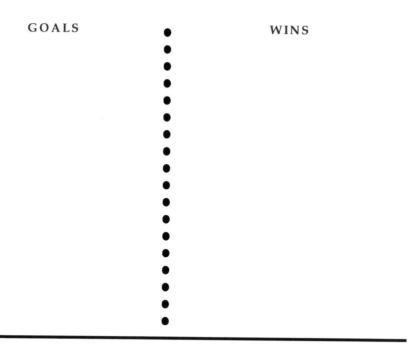

GOALS

WINS

(personal application)

MONDAY

TUESDAY

WEDNESDAY

THURSDAY

FRIDAY

SATURDAY

SUNDAY

NOTES

P.O.P. **IN** Soul

14:27 John (NLT)

"I am leaving you with a gift-- peace of mind and heart. And the peace I give is a gift the world cannot give. So, don't be troubled or afraid."

GOALS WINS

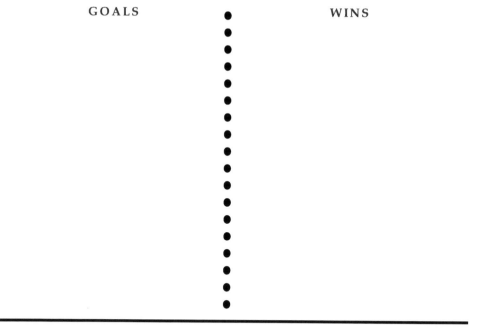

(personal application)

MONDAY

TUESDAY

WEDNESDAY

THURSDAY

FRIDAY

SATURDAY

SUNDAY

NOTES

8:9 2 Corinthians

For ye know the grace of our Lord Jesus Christ, that, though he was rich, yet for your sakes he became poor, that ye through his poverty might be rich.

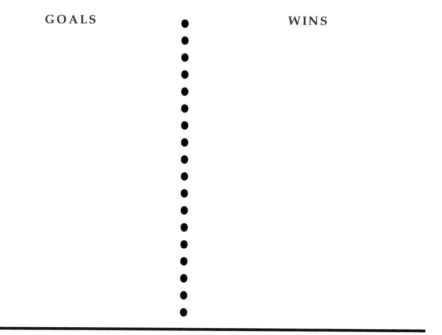

GOALS   WINS

(personal application)

MONDAY

TUESDAY

WEDNESDAY

THURSDAY

FRIDAY

SATURDAY

SUNDAY

NOTES

5:25 Ephesians

Husbands, love your wives, even as Christ also loved the church, and gave himself for it;

GOALS   WINS

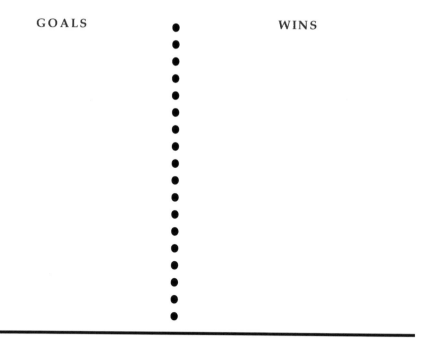

(personal application)

MONDAY

TUESDAY

WEDNESDAY

THURSDAY

FRIDAY

SATURDAY

SUNDAY

NOTES

P.O.P In Health

P.O.P.™
Prosper On Purpose

4:13 Philippians

I can do all things through Christ who strengthens me.

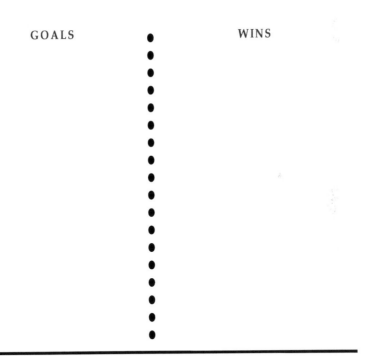

GOALS   WINS

(personal application)

MONDAY

TUESDAY

WEDNESDAY

THURSDAY

FRIDAY

SATURDAY

SUNDAY

NOTES

11:23 Mark (NLT)

I tell you the truth, you can say to this mountain, 'May you be lifted up and thrown into the sea,' and it will happen. But you must really believe it will happen and have no doubt in your heart.

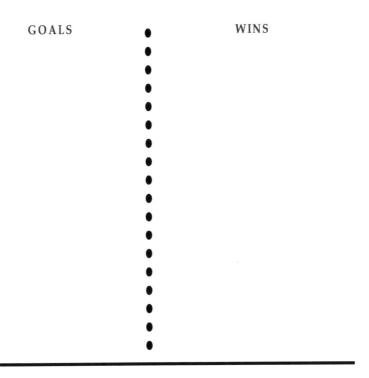

GOALS   WINS

(personal application)

MONDAY

TUESDAY

WEDNESDAY

THURSDAY

FRIDAY

SATURDAY

SUNDAY

_____

NOTES

_____

IN # Health

Exodus 23:25

And ye shall serve the Lord your God, and he shall bless thy bread, and thy water; and I will take sickness away from the midst of thee.

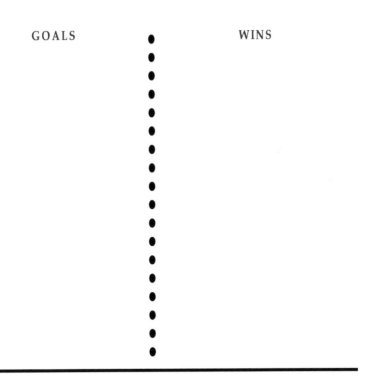

GOALS   WINS

(personal application)

MONDAY

TUESDAY

WEDNESDAY

THURSDAY

FRIDAY

SATURDAY

SUNDAY

NOTES

IN Relationships

Mark 10:8-9

The two will become one. So, they are no longer two, but one. Let no man divide what God has put together.

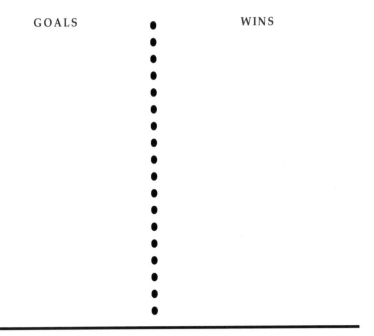

GOALS   WINS

(personal application)

MONDAY

TUESDAY

WEDNESDAY

THURSDAY

FRIDAY

SATURDAY

SUNDAY

NOTES

P.O.P.™
Prosper On Purpose

IN **Spirit**

Job (AMP) 23:25

"But there is [a vital force and] a spirit [of intelligence] in man, And the breath of the Almighty gives them understanding."

GOALS   WINS

(personal application)

MONDAY

TUESDAY

WEDNESDAY

THURSDAY

FRIDAY

SATURDAY

SUNDAY

NOTES

26:3 Isaiah

Thou wilt keep him in perfect peace, whose mind is stayed on thee: because he trusteth in thee.

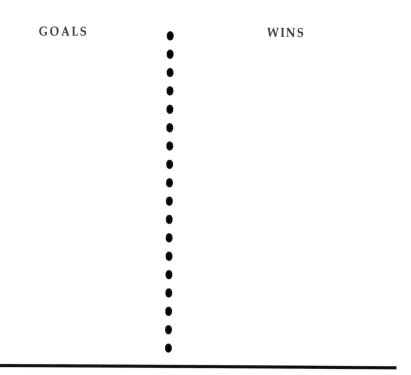

GOALS   WINS

(personal application)

MONDAY

TUESDAY

WEDNESDAY

THURSDAY

FRIDAY

SATURDAY

SUNDAY

NOTES

 IN # Health

107:20 Psalm

He sent his word, and healed them,
and delivered them from their destructions.

GOALS WINS

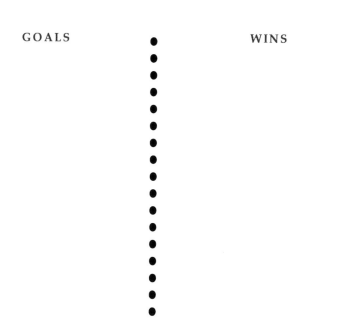

(personal application)

MONDAY

TUESDAY

WEDNESDAY

THURSDAY

FRIDAY

SATURDAY

SUNDAY

NOTES

IN Relationships

Isaiah 54:5

For thy Maker is thine husband; the Lord of hosts is his name; and thy Redeemer the Holy One of Israel; The God of the whole earth shall he be called.

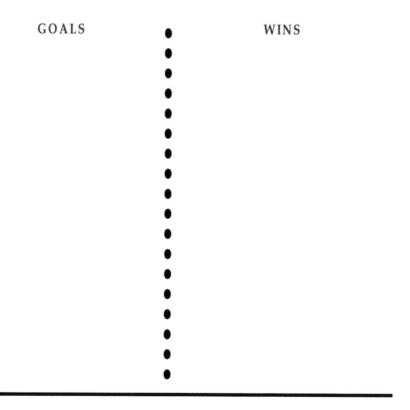

GOALS   WINS

(personal application)

MONDAY

TUESDAY

WEDNESDAY

THURSDAY

FRIDAY

SATURDAY

SUNDAY

NOTES

HOPE

P.O.P.
Prosper On Purpose

IN # Spirit

4:22 2 Timothy (NLT)

May the Lord be with your spirit. And may his grace be with all of you.

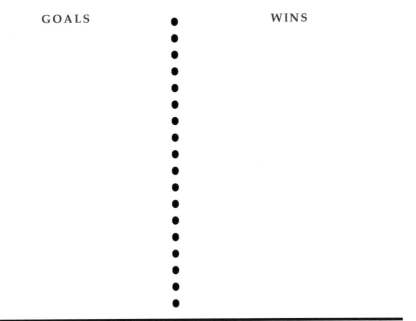

GOALS　　　　　　　　WINS

(personal application)

MONDAY

TUESDAY

WEDNESDAY

THURSDAY

FRIDAY

SATURDAY

SUNDAY

NOTES

 **IN** # Soul

John 14:1

Let not your heart be troubled: ye believe in God, believe also in me.

GOALS   WINS

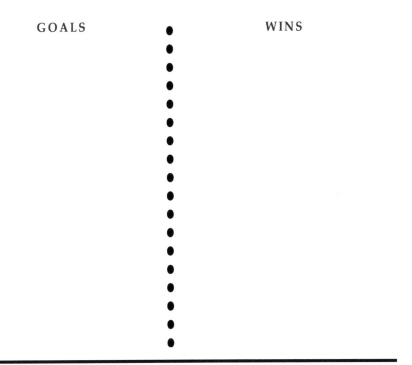

(personal application)

MONDAY

TUESDAY

WEDNESDAY

THURSDAY

FRIDAY

SATURDAY

SUNDAY

NOTES

91:16 Psalm

With long life will I satisfy him, and shew him my salvation.

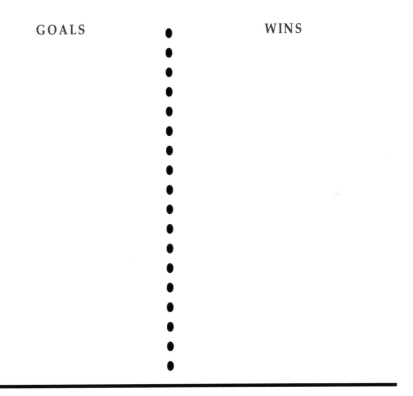

GOALS

WINS

(personal application)

MONDAY

TUESDAY

WEDNESDAY

THURSDAY

FRIDAY

SATURDAY

SUNDAY

NOTES

18:22 Proverbs

Whoso findeth a wife findeth a good thing,
and obtaineth favour of the LORD.

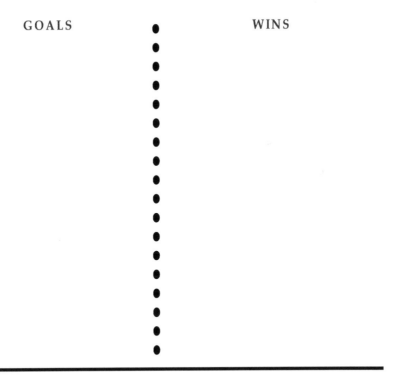

GOALS   WINS

(personal application)

MONDAY

TUESDAY

WEDNESDAY

THURSDAY

FRIDAY

SATURDAY

SUNDAY

NOTES

 IN # Spirit

1:6 Philippians (NLT)

And I am certain that God, who began the good work within you, will continue his work until it is finally finished on the day when Christ Jesus returns.

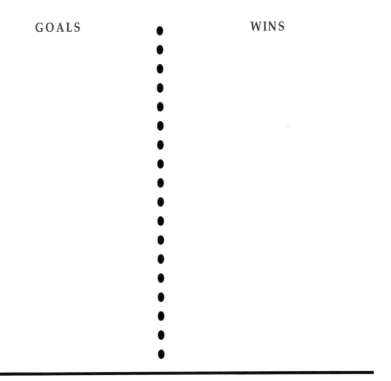

GOALS   WINS

(personal application)

MONDAY

TUESDAY

WEDNESDAY

THURSDAY

FRIDAY

SATURDAY

SUNDAY

NOTES

People don't care how much you know until they know how much you care.

- John C Maxwell

IN # Soul

16:33 John

These things I have spoken unto you, that in me ye might have peace. In the world ye shall have tribulation: but be of good cheer; I have overcome the world.

GOALS

WINS

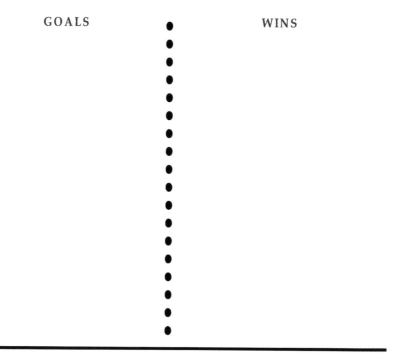

(personal application)

MONDAY

TUESDAY

WEDNESDAY

THURSDAY

FRIDAY

SATURDAY

SUNDAY

NOTES

P.O.P.™
Prosper On Purpose

IN Health

30:17a Jeremiah

*For I will restore health unto thee, and I will
heal thee of thy wounds, saith the Lord;*

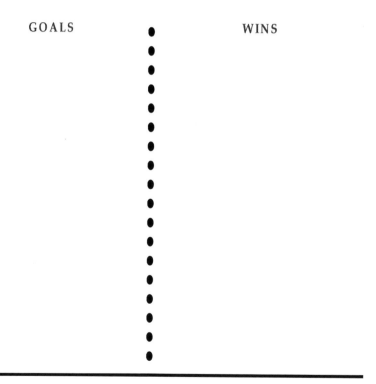

GOALS   WINS

(personal application)

MONDAY

TUESDAY

WEDNESDAY

THURSDAY

FRIDAY

SATURDAY

SUNDAY

NOTES

 **IN** Relationships

6:6 Ephesians (NLV)

Do not work hard only when your owner sees you. You would be doing this just to please men. Work as you would work for Christ. Do what God wants you to do with all your heart.

GOALS   WINS

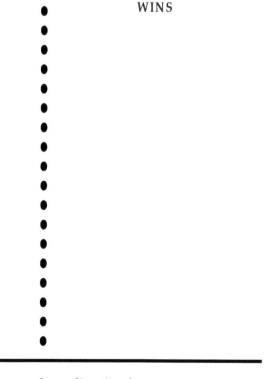

(personal application)

MONDAY

TUESDAY

WEDNESDAY

THURSDAY

FRIDAY

SATURDAY

SUNDAY

NOTES

P.O.P. ™
Prosper On Purpose

IN **Spirit**

6:10 Ephesians (NLT)

A final word: Be strong in the Lord and in his mighty power.

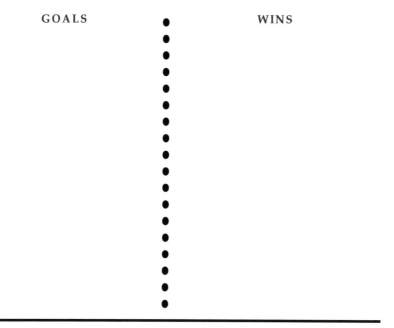

GOALS   WINS

(personal application)

MONDAY

TUESDAY

WEDNESDAY

THURSDAY

FRIDAY

SATURDAY

SUNDAY

NOTES

Prov 31:25 NLT

She is clothed with strength and dignity,
and she laughs without fear of the future

P.O.P.™
Prosper On Purpose

IN **Soul**

2:16 1 Corinthians

For who hath known the mind of the Lord, that he may instruct him?
But we have the mind of Christ.

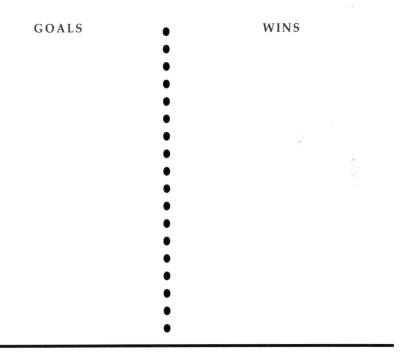

GOALS   WINS

(personal application)

MONDAY

TUESDAY

WEDNESDAY

THURSDAY

FRIDAY

SATURDAY

SUNDAY

NOTES

118:17 Psalm

I shall not die, but live, and declare the works of the Lord.

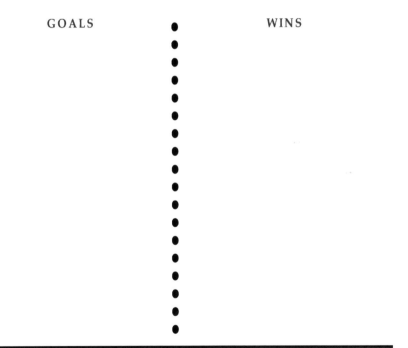

GOALS   WINS

(personal application)

MONDAY

TUESDAY

WEDNESDAY

THURSDAY

FRIDAY

SATURDAY

SUNDAY

NOTES

P.O.P.
Prosper On Purpose

IN **Finances**

DECEMBER - WEEK 3

10:22 Proverbs

The blessing of the Lord makes a person rich,
and He adds no sorrow with it.

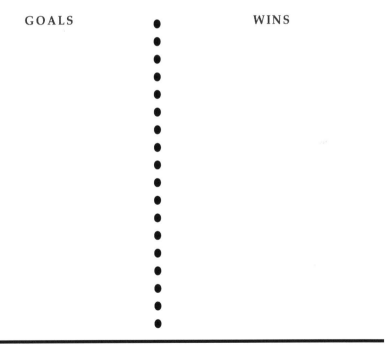

GOALS

WINS

(personal application)

MONDAY

TUESDAY

WEDNESDAY

THURSDAY

FRIDAY

SATURDAY

SUNDAY

NOTES

18:22 Proverbs

Whoso findeth a wife findeth a good thing,
and obtaineth favour of the Lord.

GOALS 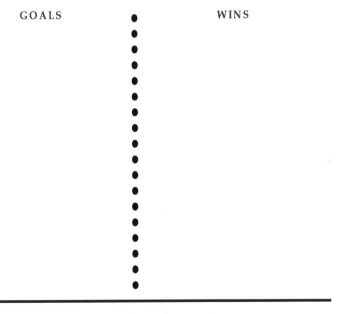 WINS

(personal application)

MONDAY

TUESDAY

WEDNESDAY

THURSDAY

FRIDAY

SATURDAY

SUNDAY

NOTES

Made in the USA
Las Vegas, NV
04 May 2021